YOU WILL ACHIEVE SUCCESS

You Will ACHIEVE SUCCESS

Read Daily for Affirmation Book Series

Walter the Educator

Silent King Books

SILENT KING BOOKS

SKB

Copyright © 2024 by Walter the Educator

All rights reserved. No part of this book may be reproduced in any manner whatsoever without written permission except in the case of brief quotations embodied in critical articles and reviews.

First Printing, 2024

Disclaimer
This book is a literary work; poems are not about specific persons, locations, situations, and/or circumstances unless mentioned in a historical context. This book is for entertainment and informational purposes only. The author and publisher offer this information without warranties expressed or implied. No matter the grounds, neither the author nor the publisher will be accountable for any losses, injuries, or other damages caused by the reader's use of this book. The use of this book acknowledges an understanding and acceptance of this disclaimer.

I pray that you ACHIEVE SUCCESS.

For where two or three are gathered together in my name, there am I in the midst of them – Matthew 18:20

YOU WILL ACHIEVE SUCCESS

No mountain high, no valley low,

You Will ACHIEVE SUCCESS

Can halt my quest, can stem my flow,

You Will ACHIEVE SUCCESS

For in my blood, a fire runs,

You Will ACHIEVE SUCCESS

A burning light, like thousand suns.

You Will ACHIEVE SUCCESS

The whispers fade, the doubts retreat,

You Will ACHIEVE SUCCESS

For in my heart, a rhythm beats,

You Will ACHIEVE SUCCESS

A pulse of hope, a song of might,

You Will ACHIEVE SUCCESS

A guiding star in darkest night.

You Will ACHIEVE SUCCESS

The world may change, the seasons turn,

You Will ACHIEVE SUCCESS

Yet in my soul, a fire will burn,

You Will ACHIEVE SUCCESS

A beacon bright, a light divine,

You Will ACHIEVE SUCCESS

"I will achieve success," it shines.

You Will ACHIEVE SUCCESS

In every breath, in every sigh,

You Will ACHIEVE SUCCESS

In every tear, in every cry,

You Will ACHIEVE SUCCESS

A promise held, a vow declared,

You Will ACHIEVE SUCCESS

A journey brave, a dream is dared.

You Will ACHIEVE SUCCESS

So let the winds of fate unfurl,

You Will ACHIEVE SUCCESS

In endless dance, in cosmic whirl,

You Will ACHIEVE SUCCESS

For in my heart, a truth is sown,

You Will ACHIEVE SUCCESS

"I will achieve success," it's known.

You Will ACHIEVE SUCCESS

The future waits, the past dissolves,

You Will ACHIEVE SUCCESS

In every step, my strength evolves,

You Will ACHIEVE SUCCESS

For in my core, a dream persists,

You Will ACHIEVE SUCCESS

A whispered vow, it still exists.

You Will ACHIEVE SUCCESS

Through every storm, through every trial,

You Will ACHIEVE SUCCESS

With every step, with every mile,

You Will ACHIEVE SUCCESS

In every fall, in every rise,

You Will ACHIEVE SUCCESS

A truth endures, a dream defies.

You Will ACHIEVE SUCCESS

The dawn will break, the shadows flee,

You Will ACHIEVE SUCCESS

A world of light, a world of free,

You Will ACHIEVE SUCCESS

With every breath, with every kiss,

You Will ACHIEVE SUCCESS

"I will achieve success," is bliss.

You Will ACHIEVE SUCCESS

In moments still, in moments fast,

You Will ACHIEVE SUCCESS

A future bright, a tethered past,

You Will ACHIEVE SUCCESS

Through every storm, through every night,

You Will ACHIEVE SUCCESS

A dream persists, a guiding light.

You Will ACHIEVE SUCCESS

So here I stand, with heart and soul,

You Will ACHIEVE SUCCESS

With every dream, with every goal,

You Will ACHIEVE SUCCESS

In every beat, in every breath,

You Will ACHIEVE SUCCESS

"I will achieve success," till death.

You Will ACHIEVE SUCCESS

Milton Keynes UK
Ingram Content Group UK Ltd.
UKHW011648130624
444169UK00015B/226